Pottery: A Handbook Of Practical Pottery For Art Teachers And Students

Richard Lunn

POTTERY

A HAND-BOOK OF
PRACTICAL POTTERY FOR
ART TEACHERS AND STUDENTS

BY

RICHARD LUNN

INSTRUCTOR AT THE ROYAL COLLEGE OF ART, SOUTH KENSINGTON

VOLUME II

DECORATION OF POTTERY

WITH 46 ILLUSTRATIONS

LONDON
CHAPMAN AND HALL, LTD.
1910

Richard Clay & Sons, Limited,
BREAD STREET HILL, E.C., AND
BUNGAY, SUFFOLK.

Printing Statement:

Due to the very old age and scarcity of this book, many of the pages may be hard to read due to the blurring of the original text, possible missing pages, missing text, dark backgrounds and other issues beyond our control.

Because this is such an important and rare work, we believe it is best to reproduce this book regardless of its original condition.

Thank you for your understanding.

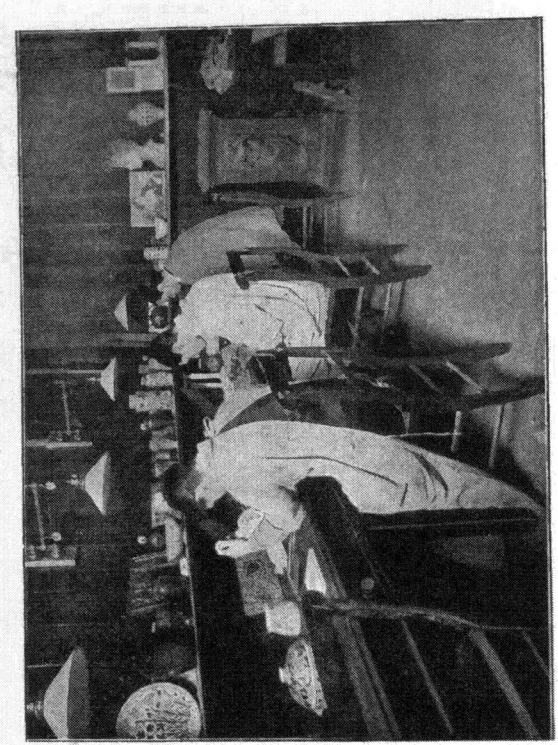

Frontispiece.

Students at work; showing arrangement of bench, shelf and electric lighting.

PREFACE

THIS volume is intended to be supplementary to the earlier handbook issued in 1903.

That volume dealt chiefly with the making of shapes, while this is mainly concerned with decoration.

The illustrations show examples of good work in the different methods described, and among them are included photographs of a few decorators at work, to show convenient arrangements of fittings, etc.

This book is primarily intended for beginners and students, and so may be found, in places, very elementary by those who know more about practical potting. It is mainly based upon teaching given by the author to practical Pottery Classes at the Royal College of Art, and other Schools of Arts and Crafts.

In conclusion I again wish to express my thanks to the officials of the Victoria and Albert Museum for their help in arranging the objects for photographing, and for reliable measurements of the ware. I also wish especially to thank Mr. G. H. Palmer for his help in revising the work.

CONTENTS

POTTERY

CHAPTER I

MATERIALS USED IN EARTHENWARE PASTES

Clays.—It may be said, generally, that the base of a clay consists of that portion of some of the minerals named felspars, which remains after their partial decomposition by atmospheric and other influences. This residue is a chemical combination of silica with alumina, and is termed silicate of alumina. In all clays it is in a hydrated form, *i. e.* it is chemically combined with water which cannot be expelled by heating the compound to the boiling-point of water.

Most clays contain, in addition to the hydrous silicate of alumina, a variable proportion of free silica and other substances in a state of mechanical (as distinguished from chemical) association with

B

them. Of such admixtures, the potash, soda, lime, or oxide of iron, which may have been present in the original felspar, are removed to a great extent in the form of soluble carbonates or bicarbonates by the action of water holding carbon dioxide (carbonic acid gas) in solution.

The manner in which a clay behaves on exposure to heat is greatly affected by these admixtures. Thus the presence of potash, lime or oxide of iron confers upon a clay a varying increase of fusibility, while additional silica renders it refractory, or difficult to fuse.

Felspars constitute a portion, often considerable, of such crystalline rocks as granite, porphyry, diorite and the like, and where such rocks exist, or have existed, clay may be found, for all felspars are liable to decomposition under certain conditions so as to yield clay-forming materials. It is observable that those species which are poorest in silica and contain much lime decompose more readily than those which are richer in silica, and contain less lime, but more soda and potash.

Kaolin or China clay.—Sometimes large masses of the decomposed remains of felspars have been carried into cavities or depressions and there covered and drifted over with other materials of the original rock. In such cases the clay is usually white, and, in this pure state, it is known as *kaolin*, from a name employed by the Chinese.

Kaolin is also obtained artificially in the following manner. A quantity of a rock which contains much quartz is exposed on an inclined plane under a fall of a few feet of water, which washes it down by degrees into a trench, whence it is conducted into catch-pits. The quartz, and the schorl, mica or other minerals which may be present, are in a great measure retained in the first catch-pit, but there is usually a second or even a third pit in which the coarser matter is collected, before the water, charged with the finer particles of the decomposed felspar, in a state of mechanical suspension, is allowed to come to rest, and deposit them in the tanks or ponds prepared for that purpose. After this deposition the water is drawn off, and the process is repeated until the tanks are nearly filled with kaolin in the state of soft clay. The clay is then removed to clay-pans heated with hot-water pipes, and, when sufficiently dry, cut into rectangular blocks. These are transferred afterwards to an artificially heated building and thoroughly dried for sale.

China stone.—The china stone of Cornwall is a disintegrated rock and consists usually of a mixture of quartz, partially decomposed felspar, and scales of greenish yellow mica. The extent to which the felspathic constituent has suffered alteration varies materially in different varieties of china stone, but it always retains more or less of its alkaline silicate and is thereby rendered more fusible. It is generally assumed that china stone is a disintegrated granitic rock, which in a more advanced state of decomposition would furnish kaolin, but the exact relationship between china stone and china clay is still somewhat obscure. China stone is quarried chiefly from the granite of St. Stephen's in Cornwall, and the quarries there furnish also some of the best kaolin.

China stone requires no preparation before being sent to the Potteries; when quarried, it is merely broken into pieces of a size convenient for carriage.

Poole clay, or Ball clay.—This clay is so named because it is shipped from Poole in Dorsetshire. It comes chiefly from the neighbourhood of Wareham. It is an example of a tolerably pure clay (that is, one containing a large proportion of silicate of alumina, with some free silica, but without injurious ingredients), which has been accumulated far from any decomposing crystalline rocks such as the granites, porphyries, etc., previously named as the frequent origin of clays. Its geological position is

EARTHENWARE PASTES

in that portion of the Tertiary or Cainozoic beds
(*i. e.* those occurring above the chalk) of Dorsetshire
and Hampshire, which corresponds with the Lower
Bagshot sands of the London district.

In the Potteries it is known as " Ball clay," and it
is made up in four qualities. The first quality is
used for tobacco pipes, the second for fine earthenware, the third for stoneware, and the fourth for the
manufacture of alum.

Flint.—This is a form of silica much used by
potters. The best flints are found in the chalk
formation, or as pebbles on the sea-shore. They
are prepared for use in the following manner. They
are calcined in kilns, and are raked out and have
water thrown over them while they are still hot.
The shattered fragments so produced are crushed
between jagged iron rollers, passed between another
finer set, and then ground with water in a revolving
mill, until the whole is a white powder, as fine as
flour.

Preparation of the above materials for use.—
Kaolin requires no preparatory cleaning, and flint is
used as it comes, finely ground, from the grinding
mills. Poole clay, which may be regarded as the
base or chief ingredient in the manufacture of
English earthenware, needs preliminary treatment.

5

POTTERY

It has to be mixed with water and reduced to a state in which it can be passed through a phosphor bronze sieve (No. 40), so as to free it from lumps and render it of a fine, uniform consistency. China stone has, too, to be crushed and reduced to a fine powder in mills. It is treated like the flints, except that it does not require calcination.

CHAPTER II

COMPOSITION OF EARTHENWARE BODIES OR PASTES

White Earthenware.—Common paste for ordinary white earthenware is generally composed of Ball clay (Dorset or Poole clay); Cornish or Devon clay, or Kaolin (China clay); and Flint. In the best paste, Cornish china stone is also used.

All the constituent materials having been prepared for use, as described in the last chapter, the proportions of each required for the kind of ware to be made are mixed together, in water, and passed through a No. 40 sieve into a tub. When the contents have been allowed to settle, the clear water on the top is drawn off with a syphon, and the residue allowed to dry. The drying may be accelerated with gentle heat if a set pot or copper is used instead of a tub. If the clay is to be used for casting, not much evaporation will be required, but if it is to be thrown or pressed, the drying must be

7

POTTERY

continued until the clay is of the consistency of soft dough. Finally, before it is used, it must be wedged, *i. e.* cut up and beaten until it is of the same consistency all through, and quite free from air-holes (see *Pottery*, Vol. I., p. 62).

Recipes.—The following are recipes for the composition of white earthenware pastes :—

Crown paste, 1st recipe,

10½ parts of ball clay,	7 parts of calcined flint,
12 parts of china clay,	4 parts of china stone.

Crown paste, 2nd recipe,

100 parts of china clay,	60 parts of china stone.
80 parts of calcined flint,	

Common CC paste,

72 parts of china clay,	84 parts of blue ball clay,
18 parts of china stone,	36 parts of calcined flint.

3½ ounces of oxide of cobalt must be added to 105 quarts of slip, as a stain to counteract the natural yellowness of the clay.

Red Earthenware is made with the natural red clay (which owes its colour to the presence of oxides of iron), after it has been sieved to rid it of pebbles and lumps of any kind. Ten per cent. of calcined flint is sometimes added to improve the paste.

EARTHENWARE

If a common CC paste and a red paste are required, which will contract evenly, they may be prepared as follows :—

50 parts of common CC   50 parts of red clay,
    paste,
 5 parts of ground felspar,   5 parts of ground flint.

Tiles.—To make white tiles, add 3 parts of sand (not finely ground) to 8 parts of common CC paste, and for red tiles, add one part of flint to 50 parts of red clay.

Terracotta.—Terracotta similar to that used in the frieze, etc., of the Quadrangle of the Victoria and Albert Museum is thus made :—

50 parts of best red clay,   1 part of flint.

The buff-coloured mouldings, etc., of the Royal Albert Hall, the Natural History Museum, and the upper part of the Imperial College of Science building, adjoining the Museum in Exhibition Road, are of a natural terracotta from the works of Messrs. Gibbs and Canning, at Tamworth in Staffordshire. The terracotta of the lower part of the Imperial College building, above referred to, is "doctored," *i. e.* the natural clay has been mixed with "grog," or fired clay finely ground. This "doctoring" reduces both the contraction when drying and the tendency to warp in the firing, but it gives the terracotta a porous surface, so that the London atmosphere soon attacks it and causes decay.

Other Bodies.—The following are useful recipes for the composition of other special pastes :—

Old Majolica paste,

260 parts of red clay, 10 parts of flint.
72 parts of common clay,

Parian paste,

11 parts of stone, 8 parts of china clay.
10 parts of felspar,

Stourbridge fire clay,

65·10 parts of silica, 7·10 parts of water (combined),
22·22 parts of alumina,
·18 parts of potash, 2·18 parts of water (hygroscopic, or which would be driven off at the temperature of boiling water),
·14 parts of lime,
·18 parts of magnesia,
1·92 parts of protoxide of iron,
·06 parts of phosphoric acid. ·58 parts of organic matter.

Ironstone,

2 parts of china stone, 1 part of flint,
2 parts of blue ball clay, 1 part of calx (calcined spar lime or chalk).
1½ parts of china clay,

Cheap paste to fire at a low heat (cone 010) and going down in 2¾ hours,

16 parts of damp clay, 4 parts of whiting.

EARTHENWARE

The heat at which this last body fires is very low ; porcelain, which fires at 1330° Centigrade, requires cone 10. It will be noticed that damp clay is specified in this last recipe. In the others dry clay is required, and in weighing out the materials allowance must be made for the 15 per cent. of moisture contained in the clays as they are delivered from the clay merchant.

CHAPTER III

POTTERY DECORATION: BRUSHES, MEDIUMS, AND COLOURS

THE making and firing of shapes having been fully described in the author's earlier handbook (*Pottery*, Vol. I., 1903), to which reference has already been made, it is possible to proceed at once, here, to describe methods of decoration. These group themselves under three heads: underglaze decoration, glazes, and overglaze decoration, and they will be dealt with in that order after this short chapter on the brushes and medium used by pottery decorators.

Brushes.—Brushes for pottery decoration are made of camel hair, and the most useful sizes are:—

as tracers	No. 2299, No. 1	. 7/6 gross,	-/8 doz.
as pointed shaders	„ 2297, No. 8	. 20/- „	2/6 doz.
as square shaders	„ 2298, No. 8	. 20/- „	2/6 doz.
as square liners			
(for Majolica)	„ 2301, No. 8	. 20/- „	2/6 doz.
as writing pencils	„ 1303, Nos. 1–8	. 12/- „	1/2 doz.

The price of pencil sticks is 3/- a gross.

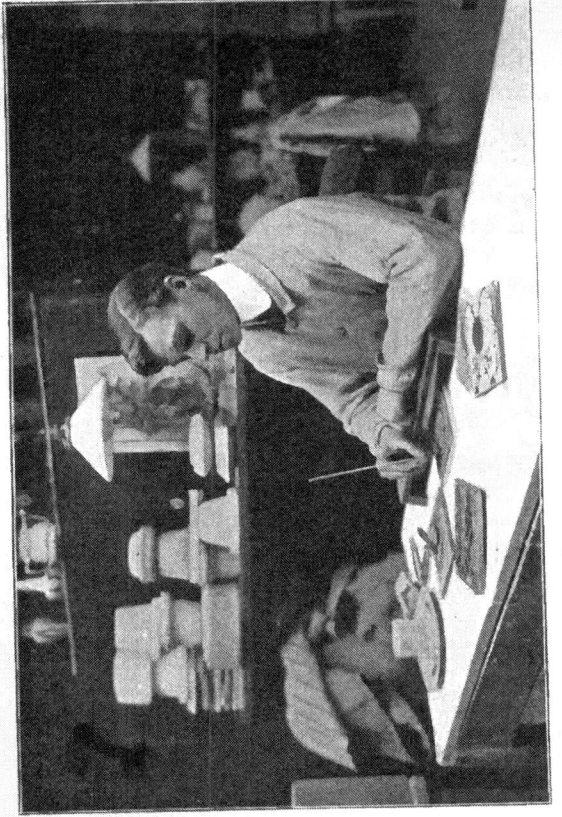

Painting tiles ; showing use of hand-rest.

13

POTTERY

Brushes should be cleaned, as follows, after use. Dip them into fresh turpentine, wash out all the colour left in them, wipe them with a clean rag, and complete the cleaning with soap and water under a tap, as when cleaning oil-colour brushes.

Brushes may be kept soft by dipping them into oil of aniseed, wiping them afterwards with a clean rag. When not in use they should be placed on a wooden rest to keep them from touching the bench, where they would gather up the dust. A convenient size is a block 6″ long and ½″ square, with a tack at each end to prevent them from rolling off.

Mediums.—The best medium for painted decoration is pure fat oil of turpentine, used neither too thin nor too thick. If used "thin," that is, with too much turpentine, it works "hard" and dries too quickly, while, if used "thick" or with too small a proportion of turpentine and too big a one of the fat oil, it works "cloggy" and stops in patches, which are very difficult to alter afterwards. It is therefore essential to use it in a middle state, *i.e.* in proper proportions.

Fat oil of turpentine should never be bought, but prepared by the student, as follows. Take a glazed plate 8″ in diameter, and a tea cup and saucer, also glazed. Place the saucer upon the plate and the cup on the saucer. Fill the cup about three parts full of best turpentine, slop a little over into the saucer, and put them all in a warm, dry place. The turpentine in the cup will soon travel up the inside of the cup, and down the outside, into the saucer. As it is doing this the spirit of the turpentine evaporates, and the fat oil alone collects in the saucer.

When the medium is being used, the greatest care is necessary that a dirty brush or a dirty palette knife should never be put into the saucer. Doing this would spoil the oil for future use.

This caution does not refer to the turpentine in the cup, for any colour or dirt getting into that soon sinks to the bottom leaving clear turpentine at the top, which can be poured off at any time into a clean vessel, and poured back again when the dirt has been wiped out with a rag or cotton waste.

When the fat oil accumulates more quickly than it is required, the surplus should be poured into a glass jar with a stopper or cork and carefully preserved for future use.

Another medium used by some pottery decorators is formed of half an ounce of gum arabic dissolved in half a pint of warm water, with a drop or two of oil of cloves added to keep it from going mouldy.

POTTERY

In conclusion, it may be mentioned that oil of aniseed is useful for getting a level ground.

Colours.—Colours are supplied by colour makers in a powdered state. They should be kept in round stoneware or glass jars, with covers, a useful size being 4″ high and 3″ in diameter. When preparing colour for use, take from the colour jar about half a scruple (= ten grains) of colour, and place it upon the glazed tile used as a palette. With a *clean* knife take up from the saucer about the same bulk of fat oil, mix it into the colour, and then dip the knife into the cup of turpentine and convey as much of this as possible to the mixture of fat oil and colour, repeat this two or three times, and then with the knife grind all together until they are well mixed and will work freely upon the ware.

It is most important for a student to remember in this connection that *a small quantity of colour goes a long way*.

When, notwithstanding this caution, some colour remains on the palette after working, a little oil of aniseed should be mixed with it before it is put away. This will keep it soft for subsequent use.

In the concluding chapter of this handbook some notes will be given on the composition of the chief colours used in pottery decoration.

CHAPTER IV

HOW TO KEEP PIECES IN POSITION WHEN THEY ARE BEING PAINTED

WHEN tiles or shapes are being painted, they must be held in such a way that they are always below the hand of the decorator. This lower position aids the flow of colour from the brush.

The tile or shape must be held in the left hand and pressed firmly against the bench, the right arm is rested on the bench, and so supported, while the wrist and hand project so as to be quite free for working.

If a shape has a great deal of pattern so that it cannot be safely held in the hand, a stick four inches longer than itself may be placed inside it and made fast by packing it in with rag or cotton waste. Grasping this stick with the left hand, it is easy to hold the shape in position against the bench; or, if necessary for convenience in working, the position may be reversed and the stick rested against the bench while the base of the shape is grasped in the left hand.

Another way to support the shape is to slip it over a bent rod of iron, inserted for that purpose into the front of the bench, and wrapped in rag to prevent damage by concussion.

A very useful height for the bench is 2 ft. 4 ins., and a good width, 2 ft.

CHAPTER V

UNDERGLAZE DECORATION

Preparation of biscuit shapes for decoration.
—At the very beginning, a word of caution is necessary. Biscuit shapes must be wrapped in clean, thin paper as soon as they are taken from the kiln, as they might otherwise be handled with warm hands and made slightly greasy, which would cause much trouble when the work of decorating began. Before any decoration is commenced, the shape must be tested. This can be done by placing the tongue on it. If the tongue adheres to the biscuit, the ware is "short," or under-fired, and the piece must be re-placed in the kiln and fired again to a proper heat, for, if glaze is placed upon "short" biscuit, it cracks and crazes when it is fired.

Even in well-fired ware, there is always a certain amount of suction, which must be modified by the application of a solution of gum tragacanth,[1]

---

[1] Tragacanth is a thorny plant growing in Greece, Africa and the East, which yields the yellowish gum named from it.

Student decorating a Vase ; showing the use of bench, easel, and rest-stick.

UNDERGLAZE DECORATION

before painting upon it is begun. The solution is thus prepared. 40 grains (2 scruples) of the gum are soaked with warm water, 3 ounces of alcohol are added, and all is ground into a thin paste, which is then stirred into a pint of warm water. One or two drops of oil of cloves should be added to the mixture to keep it from going mouldy.

With this solution—using a broad camel-hair brush—go over the biscuit surface quickly, let it dry, and repeat the process, brushing in a different direction. When the second coat is dry, test the surface with the tip of the tongue. If the latter does not adhere at all, suction is stopped and the surface is ready to receive painting. If it adheres at all, another coat must be applied. Two or more thin coats should be given rather than a thick one. The latter would almost certainly be uneven, and if tragacanth is applied unevenly, the thick parts crack and peel off, bringing the painting with them.

Preliminary sketch-outline of design.—After its treatment with tragacanth the surface should be like parchment, or prepared canvas, and as easy to paint upon. It may be drawn upon with a lead pencil, but the pencil used must be of good quality. Marks made with a cheap pencil fire on and leave a red line.

POTTERY

To sketch the design, it is safest and best to use Indian ink mixed with water. Here again a good quality must be used, as a cheap ink is liable to fire on, like a cheap pencil, and leave a red stain. The ink should be mixed with a little water and allowed to dry. It is taken up then, for use, in small quantities, with a damp brush.

When lustres are to be used, great care must be taken to have the ink thin.

Diagram of colours.—Before beginning to paint, a student must make for himself a diagram of colours, which will show him the result of firing each colour that he wishes to use, and save him much time and worry in his future work. This diagram is made as follows : a tile (6″ square) is prepared with gum tragacanth, as described above, and divided into twelve spaces. Some of each colour which it is intended to use should be placed in each of these spaces, gradated from light to dark, and fired. It should be lettered or numbered and a description of it entered in a special note-book kept for that purpose and always available for reference.

Painting-room temperature.—The painting-room must be kept warm and at as even a temperature as possible (about 60°—65° Fahr.). If it is

22

UNDERGLAZE DECORATION

allowed to become cold, the fat oil medium is chilled and will not work freely.

Painting outlines.—Outlines should be painted on first, working as follows. Put the tracer into the colour, and roll it over in it until it is full. Having placed it then upon the biscuit shape, with a quarter of an inch of its length resting upon the surface, draw it along the track of the desired outline, when the colour will be taken from the tracer and deposited upon the ware. The outlines must then be dried.

Drying.—This process may be expedited by placing the piece near a hot stove, but neither shape nor tile should be placed directly upon the stove. Printer's bits, stilts, or saddles, must always be placed first upon the stove, and the ware upon them, so that air is allowed to pass between the stove and the ware. Otherwise ware is liable to be cracked by the heat coming too suddenly upon it.

Laying flat tints with a brush.—To do this the colour must be mixed with turpentine and fat oil upon a glazed tile, just as water-colours are mixed, but it must not be made so sloppy. It is necessary to work quickly when laying on the colour, in that way almost as flat a tint can be got as by ground-laying. If it is desirable to go over the work two or three times, it is necessary to begin with almost

POTTERY

all turpentine, which has to be slopped on until the tint is even. Each application must be allowed to dry before the next is laid, otherwise the earlier will work up into the later and produce a disagreeable unevenness. A student must remember to paint thinly, as it is always easier to strengthen a tint and re-fire, than to lower a tone that is too dark.

Painting on shadows, etc.—When the earlier work is dry, pointed or square shaders must be used to paint on the shadows and local colour.

Corrections.—Any lint or any lump appearing on the painting must be removed at the end with a sharp knife or razor. A mistake made while painting on biscuit is not easily remedied. It must be washed out, as soon as possible, with turpentine, using a clean cotton rag. If any stain remains on drying, the place must be rubbed gently with sand paper, or corundum stick, care being taken not to make a depression in the surface by rubbing too hard.

Hardening-on.—Each piece should, as its painting is completed, be lightly covered with a clean cotton rag, or thin paper, and placed where it will be free from dust until the hardening-on can be done. When ready for this process it is necessary to proceed as follows. Put the saddles and stilts in the kiln and place the ware upon them, taking care to keep them away from the sides and ends of the muffle. Light all the burners and fire slowly until all is red, when the fat oil medium will be consumed (time, about $1\frac{3}{4}$ hours; cone 015). At the end of the time named turn off the gas; push in the dampers; pull up the air regulator; turn off all taps and replace the sheet-iron over the burners (if a false bottom to the kiln is not used). The cooling will then take about 7 hours.

When the time has come to take the ware from the kiln, it must be remembered that the medium has gone in the firing, so that the decoration will easily rub off or get smeared. The pieces must consequently be placed where they will be free from dust, and from all risk of being touched or handled until they are glazed.

The ware is now ready for glazing, for the hardening-on fire will have destroyed the gum tragacanth, as well as the fat oil medium, and restored the suction of the biscuit.

N.B. **Unfired shapes and tiles** can be decorated in the same way and with the same colours and mediums, as the fired, or biscuit ware, but extra care has to be taken with it as it is so fragile and so easily damaged.

CHAPTER VI

GLAZES

The process of glazing having been described in the earlier handbook (see pp. 46, *et seq.*), it is not dealt with again here, but some useful recipes for glazes will now be given.

Egyptian glaze.—This consisted of silica in the form of sand and soda, the latter probably obtained from the soda lakes in the oasis of Ammon [1] (whence comes the name of sal-ammoniac). The sand and soda were placed in a crucible in the following proportions : 20 parts of sand to 15 parts of soda ; the crucible was then put in a kiln and fired until the components just melted and ran

[1] Native soda occurs also in the mineral waters of Karlsbad, Aix, Vichy and the geysers of Iceland, also in the Caspian and Black Seas, and in California. Soda is obtainable too from the ash of plants growing near the sea, and from kelp, a kind of sea-weed. Soda made from plants is imported from Spain and France, but only to a trifling amount. Almost all our soda is manufactured from common salt, acted upon by sulphuric acid.

GLAZES

together, that is, until all bubbling had ceased. The frit so obtained was ground very fine, mixed with water and applied to the ware.

To turn it into a blue frit, three parts of cupric oxide (CuO—black oxide of copper) have to be added; while for a green frit, it is necessary to add 3 parts of cuprous oxide (Cu_2O—red oxide of copper).

Raw (*i. e.* **unfritted**) **lead glazes**.—1st recipe, for ordinary earthenware :—

66 parts of carbonate of lead,

22 parts of china stone,
12 parts of flint.

2nd recipe,

72 parts of china stone,
24 parts of flint,
120 parts of white lead (the proportion of the white

lead may be increased to 130 parts, if necessary).

3rd recipe,

100 parts of felspar, or china stone,

110 parts of white lead,
10 parts of whiting.

These glazes only require to be mixed with water and passed through a phosphor bronze sieve, No. 200, before they are ready for use.

Fritted lead glazes (fritted means imperfectly fused—run down—as described in the account of

27

POTTERY

the preparation of the frit for Egyptian glaze above).

1st recipe,

34 parts of china stone,	15 parts of flint,
17 parts of chalk,	34 parts of borax.

The above have to be fritted in a glost kiln at 1010° Centigrade (cone 07). 69 parts of the frit so prepared have then to be ground up with 10 parts of china stone and 21 parts of white lead, to make the glaze.

2nd recipe, for best CC glaze,

80 parts of borax,	50 parts of china stone,
50 parts of flint,	20 parts of whiting.

Frit these together, as the first recipe, and grind up the frit with 91 parts of china stone, 15 parts of flint, and 190 parts of white lead.

If the glaze is for Dipping it must be mixed so as to weigh 26 or 27 ounces to the pint.

Boracic acid glaze.

40 parts of boracic acid,	30 parts of flint,
40 parts of whiting,	10 parts of china clay.
50 parts of china stone,	

Frit these in a glost kiln at the same temperature as the glazes previously described, and grind up

GLAZES

200 parts of the frit with 50 parts of china stone, 40 parts of white lead, and 2 parts of borax.

Tin glaze.—This opaque glaze is made by grinding up 1 part of oxide of tin with 5 parts of either of the glazes described above, so that it will pass through a phosphor bronze sieve, No. 200. Half the above-named proportion of tin may also be used. Tin glazes were used in very early times by Persian, Moorish, and Italian potters, and special mention must be made of their use by the famous Della Robbia family.

Alkaline glaze.

20 parts of sand (silica);   15 parts of sodium carbonate.

Salt glaze.—Salt glaze requires a very high temperature in firing. Common salt (sodium chloride) is thrown into the back part of the firing holes of the oven. It is there volatilized by the heat of the fires, finds its way as a vapour into the oven, and settles upon every exposed surface. The vapour of sodium chloride and the silica in the paste of the ware react upon one another, forming hydrochloric acid, which passes off in a state of vapour, and a thin layer of sodium silicate (or soda glass), which is left as a glaze, coating the surface of the ware.

POTTERY

Coloured glazes.—Coloured glazes are prepared by the addition of the metallic colours used in pottery decoration to the glazes described above. The colour must be mixed with warm water and passed through a phosphor bronze lawn sieve, No. 200. It is then added to the glaze and the whole is passed through the sieve again. Coloured glazes are applied to the ware either by dipping or by spraying. A detailed description of "spraying" will be given in the next chapter.

When raised outline tiles are to be coloured Majolica pencils Nos. 1 and 8 should be used. Generally, the camel-hair brushes should be larger than those used in underglaze decorating.

Glazes for special colours.—The soft boracic glaze No. 321 (of which the composition is given on p. 28) is specially recommended for giving good results with the following colours :—

No. 8, crimson,
  „ 363, soft crimson,
  „ 105, pink or rose,
  „ 303, rose pompadour,
  „ 247, rose pink,
  „ 249, lilac or mauve,
  „ 414, opaque lilac,
  „ 415, dark purple,
  „ 416, light purple,

No. 427, transparent orange,
  „ 426, Indian orange,
  „ 428, bitumen brown,
  „ 82, chestnut brown,
  „ 390, chocolate,
  „ 36, purple brown,
  „ 5, Vandyke brown,
  „ 47, russet brown,
  „ 260, chamois,

GLAZES

No. 14, silk violet,
  „ 447, Hyde Park green,
  „ 254, opaque yellow,
  „ 200, canary yellow,
  „ 157, golden yellow,
  „ 292, saffron yellow,
  „ 5, amber,
  „ 255, opaque orange,

No. 261, dark brown,
  „ 262, red brown,
  „ 235, red (sang de bœuf),
  „ 81, Persian red,
  „ 280, poppy red,
  „ 400, golden red,
  „ 448, ivory white,
  „ 155, cream white,

that is, for crimsons, pinks, lilacs, purples, yellows, oranges, silk violet, Hyde Park green, and nine different browns.

The soft alkaline glaze, No. 9 (of which the composition is described on p. 29), should be used for all violets (except No. 14 GS, silk violet), all blues (including turquoise), all greens (except No. 447 M, Hyde Park green), all blacks, all greys, for the browns not specified in the preceding list, and for one yellow (No. 13 M, Roman yellow).

Opaque white glaze No. 262 should be used with the oxide turquoise, No. 422.

CHAPTER VII

ENAMEL OR OVERGLAZE DECORATION

The same metallic colours are used for overglaze painting as for underglaze, but for overglaze painting flux has to be mixed with them. The use of the flux is to make them fire on at a much lower heat, *i. e.* at 860° Centigrade (cone 013), while underglaze colours require 1010° Centigrade (cone 07).

The fluxes used in pottery decoration are very various, and distinguished by different names, but they almost always consist of litharge or red lead (with the addition of sand or boracic acid), or of both those substances together. The fluxes are essentially colourless glasses used as vehicles for the infusible colours.

A useful flux is that known as No. 8 flux, of which the composition is as follows :—

6 parts of red lead,   2 parts of flint.
4 parts of borax,

For use three or four parts of this flux have to

Lining Wheel and Arm-rest ; showing manner of putting lines and bands
of colour upon a plate.

be added to one part of colour. When they are so mixed, the colour and flux must be ground together with a muller upon a glass slab.

The colours should be used just as underglaze colours are. A thin coat should first be applied, which may be followed by a much thicker second. It is a good plan to dry the pieces in an enamel or a hardening-on kiln, as this to a great extent prevents the colours running.

A useful palette for small quantities of mixed colours is a $3'' \times 3'' \times \frac{1}{2}''$ slab, with 9 circular holes in it, and a cardboard cover to protect it from dust.

One great advantage of overglaze painting is that mistakes can be easily remedied. The colour can be wiped off and a fresh start made, without any stain being left to trouble the decorator, as would be the case in underglaze painting.

As in underglaze work, great care must be taken to keep the fat oil medium, brushes, rag, bench and other accessaries, as well as the palette and colours, quite clean and free from dust. If there were any dust on the decoration when it was fired, it would make it very unsightly. If it gets there at all, it must be cut off, when dry, with a very sharp knife or razor, before the firing, or next painting. Lint is almost more troublesome still, as it gathers the

colour round it, and causes, if not cut off, a dark
lump of colour when the firing is completed. This
lump would have to be rubbed down with corundum
stick. On this account old silk should be used for
the rag, as it is free from lint.

A further advantage of overglaze work is that
highly finished painting does not lose its detail
when fired at the low heat required. Fine examples of overglaze decoration may be seen in
Italian Majolica, examples of which are illustrated
on pages 65 to 70.

Nearly all decoration on porcelain is "overglaze."
Cobalt used to be worked "underglaze," but it is now
used over the glaze and fired at a heat almost as
great as glost. This causes the colour to sink into
the glaze, and it is less liable to run.

Speaking generally, turquoise is always more
successful when used "overglaze," and bright and
rich reds can be so obtained which would be im-
possible "underglaze." If a particularly brilliant red
is required, the biscuit should first be painted with
underglaze yellow, glazed and fired (cone 07), and
then receive overglaze red and be fired in the enamel
kiln (cone 013). Gold and lustres are also used
overglaze.

Gilding.—The following is a useful recipe :—

POTTERY

2 dwt. of best brown gold,	1½ dwt. of leaf silver or pre-
1 dwt. of mercury,	pared silver,
	3 grs. of No. 8 flux.

These have to be well ground on a glass slab with a glass muller. The composition, when ground, is applied to the ware just as colour is, with camel-hair brushes and the usual medium of fat oil and turpentine.

Another recipe is as follows :—

½ oz. of gold,	40 grs. of silver,
½ oz. of mercury,	60 grs. of bismuth.
¼ oz. of red oxide of iron,	

Lustres.—The essence of lustre painting consists in obtaining such an extremely fine film of metal that it shall seem iridescent.

To accomplish this the ceramic colours (mainly oxides) have to be mixed more or less with a bismuth base. "Bismuth glass" is the base of the lustre for all colours. It is prepared by fusing together in a crucible, 4 parts of bismuth oxide and 4 parts of crystallized boracic acid.

The preparation of lustres is a very tedious and delicate operation, so that the student will do well to procure them ready made from the ceramic colourmen.

The ware must be warmed for lustre-painting, as this causes the lustre to flow evenly.

CHAPTER VIII

GROUND-LAYING

GROUND-LAYING is so important a part of pottery decoration that it has seemed to be worth while to devote a short chapter to the ways in which it is usually done, the two most important being (1) with a dabber, and (2) by spraying.

With a dabber.—In ground-laying with a dabber, an oil is used which may be prepared by boiling together for about two hours the following ingredients :—

2 quarts of linseed oil,	1½ ounces of red lead, and
1 ounce of gum mastic,	1 pint of turpentine.

The dabber itself is made of cotton wool rolled into a ball and covered with silk, with the surplus portion of the silk tied round with twine so as to form a handle. It is necessary that the silk should be of fine, smooth, and even texture.

The first step in ground-laying is to distribute a coat of oil evenly over the surface with the dabber, taking great care to keep it clear of dust or lint. When the oil has been laid evenly and well, the oiled shape should be placed upon a tray and the colour dusted upon it with cotton wool, this process being continued until the oil will not absorb any more colour. The ware can then be fired.

If portions of the shape have to be left uncoloured, it is necessary to proceed as follows. Begin by covering those parts with a brush with common treacle. When that is *quite dry*, lay the oil over every part and dust on the colour as described above. When it is all set, immerse the shape in water and rub the treacled parts gently with cotton wool. The water will cause the treacle to swell, and will bring it away, and the oil and colour with it, so as to leave those parts of the ware clear, as required. In this process it is absolutely essential that the treacled parts should be quite dry before the laying on of the oil. For ground-laying the workroom must be warm and dry ; it is very difficult to lay a ground on a wet or foggy day.

By spraying.—Ground-laying on this plan is done in much the same way as the fixing of crayon drawings.

The coloured glaze must be mixed with gum-water and passed through a five-inch funnel sieve into a glass bottle (the passing of coloured glazes through the funnel sieve is important and must not be neglected). Into the glass bottle a sprayer is inserted. The vase to be sprayed, which must be quite clean and free from grease, is placed on a whirler and the spray is blown upon it, the whirler being turned as required. For pieces of large size a foot-blower is required, to obtain the necessary air pressure. A screen must be placed on the other side of the piece being sprayed to catch the spray that misses it.

On the glaze, with a brush.—Ground-laying can be done on the glaze, by using a large flat brush to cover the shape with coloured glaze. If a pattern is required, the parts it will occupy can be taken out with a wooden tool, and it can then be painted in, in the desired colour. Examples of such work can be seen on Italian majolica plates.

39

CHAPTER IX

SLIPS AND COLOURED PASTES, SLIP DECORATION, AND SGRAFFIATO

Preparation of slip.—To prepare slip, a lump of moist clay (about 8″ cube) must be taken and pulled into small pieces. These are placed into a galvanized iron pail, which is then filled three parts full of warm water. The pieces of clay must be squeezed and worked with both hands, more water being added as the work proceeds until the pail is nearly full and the whole contents form a "slip" of the thickness of cream. Before use it must be passed through a phosphor bronze sieve, No. 40, into another vessel.

To colour slip.—To colour the slip prepared as above, the required metallic oxide, or stain, must be mixed with warm water and added to the slip in the following proportions : (*a*) one part of oxide to about four parts of slip for dark tints, or (*b*) one part of oxide to about twenty parts of slip for light tints.

SLIPS AND COLOURED PASTES

The mixture should be passed through a phosphor bronze sieve, No. 200, after which it is ready for application to the ware.

Coloured pastes.—If the coloured slip is allowed to stand, the coloured clay will settle so that much of the water may be poured off. Further moisture may be withdrawn by pouring the residue in a wooden frame, half an inch deep, upon a dry plaster of Paris bat or slab, or it may be dried by evaporation until a coloured paste is left of the right consistency for throwing or pressing.

Slip decoration.—The covering or decorating of unfired ware with white or coloured slip may be done in several ways. Dipping may be used or spraying ; the slip may be painted on like tempera or body colour ; or a method not previously described, *i.e.* the "dip-can" and lathe, may be adopted.

The "dip-can" is a vessel with a spout of which the shape can be varied. The "dip-turner" has one of these vessels full of slip, and, by blowing into it through another tube, he forces the slip out upon the piece to be decorated, which is meanwhile slowly revolved upon the lathe. In this way rings of slip, only, may be deposited, or the whole shape may be covered. Further patterns can be formed

POTTERY

on the slip, by depositing on it slips of other colours before it becomes dry.

Shapes decorated with slip decoration are dried, and fired in the biscuit kiln in the usual way.

Sgraffiato.—A clay shape, which is to be decorated in this way, is first covered, while still damp, with a thin coating of slip of another colour, applied with a brush or by spraying. When this coating is set, but while it is still damp, the design must be transferred upon it, and the ground or ornament cut away with a steel tool so that the pattern is displayed in the different colours of the shape and of the coating laid upon it. Red clay is frequently used for the shape, and a light-coloured clay for the outer coating.

Care must be taken that the shape is not too dry before the other clay is spread upon it, or it may crack and be spoiled. Afterwards the piece must be kept in the damp bin until all the work upon it is finished. If, notwithstanding this precaution, the outer coating becomes too dry, so that it chips or flakes off when cut with the tool, the part to be worked upon must be moistened by blowing a slight spray of water over it, or by damping it with a wet camel-hair brush.

Here again caution is necessary, as too much

42

moisture may weaken the part so much that it will collapse and fall away.

When the decoration is complete and the whole is dry, the shape must be fired and then glazed with a plain or coloured glaze, as desired.

CHAPTER X

NOTES ON THE BASIS OF SOME OF THE CHIEF CERAMIC COLOURS

THE colours used in pottery decoration are almost all derived from minerals, and they are mostly oxides of different metals.

The most important of these metallic oxides are :—

oxide of cobalt, which is used chiefly in the preparation of blues, greys and blacks, all capable of standing a high temperature in firing ;

oxide of chromium, which produces a very stable green ;

peroxide of iron, or ferric oxide, which is used for reds, browns and violets, the tints varying with the temperature at which calcination is effected, and capable of modification by mixing with other oxides ;

oxide of antimony, which gives various shades of yellow. It is generally mixed with oxide of zinc or oxide of iron, but sometimes we have it combined instead to form antimoniate of lead, or Naples yellow ;

44

CERAMIC COLOURS

oxides of copper, which form silicates of two colours :
(1) red, with the sub-oxide (cuprous salts), and (2) blue
with the protoxide (cupric salts), when they are
associated with an alkaline silicate ;

peroxide of manganese, which is used for violets and
blacks, and occurs abundantly in a native state as
" pyrolusite " ;

sesquioxide of uranium, a rare compound, which is
occasionally employed to produce an orange colour;
and

oxide of iridium, an expensive preparation which is
highly valued for producing a black of extraordinary
intensity.

Oxide of zinc is incapable by itself of imparting
colour to any vitreous substance, but it is of great
value on account of its power of modifying and
improving colours with which it may be used, such
as the cobalt blues.

As has been explained these colouring materials
are used with fluxes. The flux employed may often
affect the tint. The chief materials used for fluxing
are felspar, borax, nitre, litharge, alkaline carbonates
and preparations of bismuth. The composition of
some fluxes that can be recommended has been
detailed in Chapter VII. One point that has to be
carefully attended to is that the vitreous substance
formed by the metallic oxides and the flux must
expand and contract by alterations of temperature,

absolutely uniformly with the paste or glaze to which they are applied. Otherwise cracking or crazing will result.

Note on firing.—Instructions to fire ware in a

Gas Muffle Kiln, showing the manner of placing the ware in the Muffle.

biscuit kiln, a glost kiln, or an enamel kiln, or in all successively, does not mean that three separate muffle kilns are required. The same kiln (a gas muffle kiln, $18'' \times 14'' \times 14''$, is recommended) may be used in each case, the above quoted terms are only to describe briefly the temperature and duration of firing.

" Biscuit kiln " means firing at cone 03 (or 1*a*), seven hours being required ; glost kiln, at cone 07 (or 05*a*), four hours being necessary ; enamel kiln, at cone 013, for two hours.

FIG. 1.——Vase. Chinese porcelain. Brown
ground, white panel with blue ornament. Height 7¼ ins., diameter 4⅝ ins.

FIG. 2.——Vase. Syrian, 15th century. Height
12¼ ins., diameter 8⅞ ins.

48

FIG. 3.—Jar. Persian, 16th or 17th century.
Height 7¾ ins., diameter 8¼ ins.

FIG. 4.—Bowl. Persian, 19th century. Perforated pattern filled with
glaze. Height 3⅞ ins., diameter 9 ins.

Fig. 5.—Bowl. Persian, 17th or 18th century. Perforations filled with glaze. Height 3½ ins., diameter 7½ ins.

Fig. 6.—Bowl. Persian, 17th or 18th century. Perforated pattern filled with glaze. Height 3⅝ ins., diameter 8¼ ins.

FIG. 7.—Bowl. Damascus, 16th century. Height 11 ins., diameter 17 ins.

FIG. 8.—Bowl. Damascus, 16th century. Height 10¾ ins., diameter 16¾ ins.

FIG. 9.—Damascus, 16th century.   Height 4⅞ ins., diameter 9⅝ ins.

FIG. 10.—Tazza bowl.   Persian, 16th century.
Height 7 ins., diameter 7½ ins.

52

FIG. 11.—Dish. Damascus, 16th century. Height 3⅝ ins., diameter 14⅝ ins.

FIG. 12.—Dish. Damascus, 16th century. Height 3 ins., diameter 14¾ ins.

53

FIG. 13.—Dish. Damascus, 16th century. Height 1⅜ ins., diameter 13¼ ins.

FIG. 14.—Damascus, 16th century. Height 2⅝ ins., diameter 14¼ ins.

FIG. 15.—Body of a Vase. Syrian (Damascus), 16th century.
Height 12¼ ins., diameter 10⅞ ins.

FIG. 16.—Dish. Painted in polychrome. Damascus, 16th century.
Height 2⅝ ins., diameter 14¼ ins.

55

FIG. 17.—Vase or Bottle. Turkish, 15th or 16th
century. Height 12½ ins., diameter 7⅝ ins.

FIG. 18.—Plate ; lobed edges, painted in blue and green. Syrian
(Damascus), 16th century. Height 2⅝ ins., diameter 14⅜ ins.

56

FIG. 19.—Dish. Turkish, 16th century. Height 3½ ins., diameter 15½ ins.

FIG. 20.—Plate. Persian, 16th century lustre. Height 1¾ ins., diameter 9 ins.

57

Fig. 21.—Porcelain Plate. Blue and white. Chinese.
Height 1 in., diameter 6¼ ins.

Fig. 22.—Tiles. Damascus, 16th or 17th century. Length 2 ft. 1¼ ins., width 8¾ ins.

FIG. 23.—Tiles. Damascus, 16th or 17th century. Length 3 ft. 3¾ ins., width 14 ins.

Fig. 24.—Kalian or Pipe (Base of). Persian, 16th or
17th century. Height 6¼ ins., diameter 7 ins.

Fig. 25.—Vase. Persian, 15th century. Slip decoration.
Height 6½ ins., diameter 6¼ ins.

61

FIG. 26.—Red Earthenware Jug, in white slip
under a yellow glaze. English, 17th century.
Height 9 ins., diameter 5⅝ ins.

FIG. 27.—Bowl. Spanish Lustre (Manises, near Valencia), second
half of 17th century. Height 3½ ins., diameter 11¾ ins.

x

62

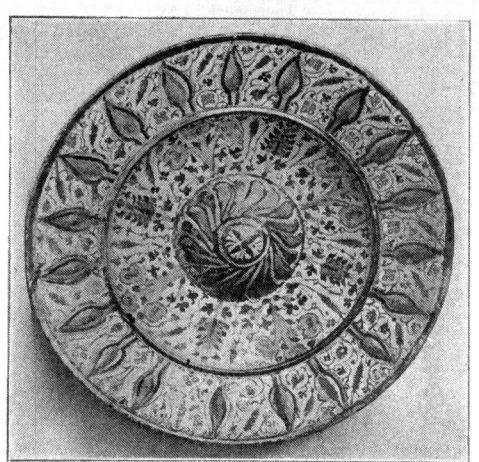

FIG. 28.—Plateau. Spanish Lustre (Valencia), 15th century.
Height 3 ins., diameter 19½ ins.

FIG. 29.—Dish. "Sgraffiato," or incised ware. Italian, late
15th century. Height 2 ins., diameter 14⅛ ins.

FIG. 30.—Dish. "Sgraffiato," or incised ware. Persian.
Height 3¼ ins., diameter 14½ ins.

FIG. 31.—Pot. "Sgraffiato," or incised ware.
Italian, 17th century. Height 9½ ins,
diameter 6⅛ ins.

FIG. 32.—Majolica Plate, lustred. Italian (Gubbio), School of Maestro Giorgio, about 1550. Height 1½ ins., diameter 9¾ ins.

FIG. 33.—Majolica Plate (sunk centre). Italian (Siena), about 1510.
Height 2 ins., diameter 8 ins.

FIG. 34.—Majolica Plate. Italian (Castel Durante), about 1510.
Height 2 in., diameter 9¾ ins.

FIG. 35.—Majolica. Flower-stand. Italian (Urbino), 16th
century. Height 8¼ ins., diameter at base 11½ ins.

FIG. 36.—Border of Majolica Plateau. Italian (Urbino), about 1560–70.
Height 2¼ ins., diameter 17½ ins.

FIG. 37.—Border of Majolica Plateau. Italian (Urbino), about 1560.
Height 2 ins., diameter 17¾ ins.

FIG. 38.—Majolica Vase. Italian (Urbino), about
1560-70. Height 22½ ins., diameter 12 ins.

FIG. 39.—Plateau. Italian (Caffaggiolo), about 1515-20.
Height 1¾ ins., diameter 15½ ins.

FIG. 40.—Plate. Italian (Caffaggiolo), about 1515-20.
Height 1¾ ins., diameter 12½ ins.

FIG. 41.—Plate. Persian (Ispahan). Height 1⅞ ins., diameter
10⅜ ins. Paris Ex. 1889.

DESCRIPTION OF ILLUSTRATIONS

ON PAGES 48 TO 70

Fig. 1.—Vase. Chinese porcelain. Height $7\frac{1}{4}$ ins., diameter $4\frac{7}{8}$ ins.

An example of ground-laying. Ground a deep brown, panel white, ornament blue.

Fig. 2.—Vase. Syrian, 15th century. Height $12\frac{1}{4}$ ins. diameter $8\frac{7}{8}$ ins.

Dark ornament (manganese), on cream-coloured ground, the leaves of light blue.

Fig. 3.—Jar. Persian, 16th or 17th century. Height $7\frac{3}{4}$ ins., diameter $8\frac{1}{4}$ ins.

A good shape for Pottery. The decoration is blue, with black outline.

Fig. 4.—Bowl. Persian, 19th century. Perforated pattern filled with glaze. Height $3\frac{7}{8}$ in., diameter 9 ins.

Blue decoration with black outline.

Fig. 5.—Bowl. Persian, 17th or 18th century. Perforations filled with glaze. Height $3\frac{1}{2}$ ins., diameter $7\frac{1}{2}$ ins.

Decoration blue, outlined with black.

Fig. 6.—Bowl. Persian, 17th or 18th century. Perforated pattern filled with glaze. Height $3\frac{5}{8}$ ins., diameter $8\frac{1}{4}$ ins.

Incised bands of ornament.

71

POTTERY

Fig. 7.—Bowl. Damascus, 16th century. Height 11 ins., diameter 17 ins.

The colours used are deep blue, turquoise-blue, manganese, pale olive-green, outline black.

Fig. 8.—Bowl. Damascus, 16th century. Height 10¾ ins., diameter 16¾ ins.

The same as No. 7.

Fig. 9.—Damascus, 16th century. Height 4⅞ ins., diameter 9⅜ ins.

Blue ground, black outline. The colours used in the ornament are grey-blue, manganese, sage-green.

Fig. 10.—Tazza bowl. Persian, 16th century. Height 7 ins., diameter 7½ ins.

Black outline. Colours used: dark-blue, manganese, and yellow-green.

Fig. 11.—Dish. Damascus, 16th century. Height 3⅝ ins., diameter 14⅝ ins.

Dark-blue ground on the rim. Colours used in the ornament are light sage-green, dark-blue, manganese, turquoise-blue; dark outline.

Fig. 12.—Dish. Damascus, 16th century. Height 3 ins., diameter 14¾ ins.

A very beautiful design. Colours used: light yellow-green, medium-blue, turquoise-blue; slight outline in yellow-green.

Fig. 13.—Dish. Damascus, 16th century. Height 1¾ ins., diameter 13¼ ins.

Colours used in the decoration are dark-blue, turquoise-blue, manganese, yellow-green, with dark outline of varying strength.

DESCRIPTION

Fig. 14.—Damascus, 16th century. Height 2⅝ ins., diameter 14¼ ins.

Dark-blue ground covering the whole of the shape. Colours used : turquoise-blue, manganese, sage-green, with black outline.

Fig. 15.—Body of a Vase. Syrian (Damascus), 16th century. Height 12¼ ins., diameter 10⅞ ins.

Medium blue ground. Colours used in the decoration are : bright light-green, manganese ; medium black outline. (Formerly the property of the late Lord Leighton, P.R.A.)

Fig. 16.—Dish. Painted in polychrome. Damascus, 16th century. Height 2⅝ ins., diameter 14¼ ins.

Ground of the rim is dark-blue. Colours used : sage-green, turquoise-blue, manganese, dark-blue, with black outline.

Fig. 17.—Vase or Bottle. Turkish, 15th or 16th century. Height 12½ ins., diameter 7⅝ ins.

Decoration, painted with flowers in red, blue and green.

Fig. 18.—Plate ; lobed edges, painted in blue and green. Syrian (Damascus), 16th century. Height 2⅝ ins., diameter 14¾ ins.

The centre and rim have a medium-blue ground. Yellow-green and turquoise-blue, with dark-blue outline, are used in the decoration.

Fig. 19.—Dish. Turkish, 16th century. Height 3½ ins., diameter 15½ ins.

Decoration : dark-blue outline filled in with medium-blue.

Fig. 20.—Plate. Persian, 16th century lustre. Height 1¾ ins., diameter 9 ins.

Light-green ground. Decoration in brown lustre.

POTTERY

Fig. 21.—Porcelain Plate. Blue and white. Chinese.
Height 1 in., diameter 6¼ ins.

Blue, with a dragon rising from the waves to a higher
existence. The rim has waves and flowers on a lined blue
ground.

Fig. 22.—Tiles. Damascus, 16th or 17th century. Length
2 ft. 1¼ ins., width 8⅞ ins.

Panel of tiles with an inscription on a dark-blue ground,
interspersed with the lettering and slight white curving
stems, flowers, and leaves, with small patches of green.

Fig. 23.—Tiles. Damascus, 16th or 17th century. Length
3 ft. 3½ ins., width 14 ins.

Panel of tiles, with inscription outlined with black, dark-
blue ground, with flowers and leaves in turquoise-blue.
The panels have a light-green ground, and the ornament
in them is white.

Fig. 24.—Kalian or Pipe (Base of). Persian, 16th or 17th
century. Height 6¼ ins., diameter 7 ins.

With raised white flowers in slip on sage-green glaze.

Fig. 25.—Vase. Persian, 15th century. Slip decoration.
Height 6½ ins., diameter 6¼ ins.

White slip decoration with orange-coloured glaze.

Fig. 26.—Red Earthenware Jug, in white slip under a
yellow glaze. English, 17th century. Height 9 ins.,
diameter 5⅝ ins.

Red clay, with white slip decoration with orange-coloured
glaze.

Fig. 27.—Bowl. Spanish Lustre (Manises, near Valencia),
second half of 17th century. Height 3⅛ ins., diameter
11⅞ ins.

DESCRIPTION

Light orange-coloured ground, decorated with copper lustre.

Fig. 28.—Plateau. Spanish Lustre (Valencia), 15th century. Height 3 ins., diameter 19½ ins.

Ivory-coloured ground, decoration in copper lustre, with raised leaves, guilloche in centre, and four ornaments on the well of the dish in light-blue.

Fig. 29.—Dish. "Sgraffiato," or incised ware. Italian, late 15th century. Height 2 ins., diameter 14⅜ ins.

Red clay, with sgraffiato decoration. The lead glaze is coloured with yellow oxide of iron, which reduces the redness of the clay.

Fig. 30.—Dish. "Sgraffiato," or incised ware. Persian. Height 3¼ ins., diameter 14½ ins.

Large plate of red clay, with sgraffiato decoration. The lead glaze is coloured with yellow oxide of iron, which reduces the redness of the clay.

Fig. 31.—Pot. "Sgraffiato," or incised ware. Italian, 17th century. Height 9½ ins., diameter 6¼ ins.

Pot, of red clay, with sgraffiato decoration. The lead glaze is coloured with yellow oxide of iron, which reduces the redness of the clay.

Fig. 32.—Majolica Plate, lustred. Italian (Gubbio), School of Maestro Giorgio, about 1550. Height 1½ ins., diameter 9⅞ ins.

Cupid painted in grisaille in the centre, on a rich ruby background, round this is a plain band of rich buff. The rim of the plate has a blue ground. The decoration has been taken out and slightly tinted. The flowers at the termination of the scrolls are a rich ruby lustre. The edge of the rim is brown.

POTTERY

Fig. 33.—Majolica Plate (sunk centre). Italian (Siena), about 1510. Height 2 ins., diameter 8 ins.

Plate. Cupid in the centre, framed with a block ornament of blue and orange. The well of the plate is light-ivory colour, with a dainty white ornament (tin). The rim has a blue ground with ornament in grey and orange. Borders of arabesques, with medallions containing emblems on an orange ground.

Fig. 34.—Majolica Plate. Italian (Castel Durante), about 1510. Height 2 ins., diameter 9⅜ ins.

Plate painted with arabesque border on blue ground, all outlined in strong blue. Shading in blue-grey and yellow. Yellow edge. Green, red, and yellow are used.

Fig. 35.—Majolica. Flower-stand. Italian (Urbino), 16th century. Height 8⅛ ins., diameter at base 11½ ins.

Flower-stand. Figures shaded with grey and yellow on a black ground. The lines framing the figures are coloured with blue, orange, and green. The lion heads and claws are orange.

Fig. 36.—Border of Majolica Plateau. Italian (Urbino), about 1560–70. Height 2¼ ins., diameter 17½ ins.

Plateau. The decoration has a dark, varying outline, shaded in light-red, yellow and grey. Medallions have black or light-blue grounds. Edge of rim is orange.

Fig. 37.—Border of Majolica Plateau. Italian (Urbino), about 1560. Height 2 ins., diameter 17¾ ins.

Plateau, ivory-coloured ground. The figures have a dark outline, and are shaded in light-red, orange and grey. Medallions have black ground.

DESCRIPTION

Fig. 38.—Majolica Vase. Italian (Urbino), about 1560–70. Height 22½ ins., diameter 12 ins.

Noticeable principally for the dexterous way in which the decoration is executed, showing a great knowledge of the human figure and animals. Shading of ornament and figures in light-red and yellow-grey, wings light-blue.

Fig. 39.—Plateau. Italian (Caffaggiolo), about 1515–20. Height 1¾ ins., diameter 15½ ins.

Plateau (Caffaggiolo). Wide arabesque border of cupids, trophies, masks, baskets of fruit, etc. Medium blue background, figures shaded in light blue-grey and yellow. Colours used are manganese, turquoise-blue, and dark-red. Well of plaque light ivory-colour ground, with white ornament (tin).

Fig. 40.—Plate. Italian (Caffaggiolo), about 1515–20. Height 1¾ ins., diameter 12½ ins.

Plate. The rim has a dark-blue ground, with the ornament taken out and slightly tinted. The well of the plate has a grey ground with dainty white ornament (tin). Cupids in the centre are in blue monochrome.

Fig. 41.—Plate. Persian (Ispahan). Height 1⅞ ins., diameter 10⅜ ins. Paris Ex. 1889.

Plate. Ivory-coloured ground, dark-blue centre and band, centre of buds also dark blue. Colours used: sage-green, turquoise-blue ; a light sage ground to outer border.